LOVE KNOWING LOVE

BOOKS BY MARTIN JANELLO

LIVE KNOWING LIFE
ISBN 978-0-9910649-6-0 (Paperback)
ISBN 978-0-9983020-2-7 (Kindle)

LOVE KNOWING LOVE
ISBN 978-0-9910649-7-7 (Paperback)
ISBN 978-0-9983020-3-4 (Kindle)

PINE KNOWING PAIN
ISBN 978-0-9910649-5-3 (Paperback)
ISBN 978-0-9983020-6-5 (Kindle)

SHINE KNOWING SHAME
ISBN 978-0-9983020-4-1 (Paperback)
ISBN 978-0-9983020-7-2 (Kindle)

CLIMB KNOWING AIM
ISBN 978-0-9983020-5-8 (Paperback)
ISBN 978-0-9983020-8-9 (Kindle)

KNOWING WON'T LET DARKNESS REIGN
ISBN 978-0-9983020-1-0 (Paperback)
ISBN 978-0-9983020-9-6 (Kindle)

PHILOSOPHY OF HAPPINESS
ISBN 978-0-9910649-0-8 (Hardcover)
ISBN 978-0-9910649-8-4 (Paperback, Pt. 1)
ISBN 978-0-9910649-9-1 (Paperback, Pt. 2)
ISBN 978-0-9910649-1-5 (PDF E-book)
ISBN 978-0-9910649-2-2 (Kindle)
ISBN 978-0-9910649-3-9 (EPUB)

PHILOSOPHIC REFLECTIONS
ISBN 978-0-9910649-4-6 (PDF E-book)

LOVE KNOWING LOVE

PHILOSOPHICAL QUOTES & POEMS

MARTIN JANELLO

Copyright © 2015 by Martin Janello
All rights reserved

No part of this book may be reproduced or transmitted,
in any form or by any means, electronic,
mechanical, or otherwise,
without prior written permission from its
copyright owner

Cover, book design, and artwork by Martin Janello

Published by Palioxis Publishing

Palioxis, Palioxis Publishing,
and the Palioxis Publishing colophon
are trademarks owned by Martin Janello

Publisher website:
www.palioxis.com

Book website:
www.philosophyofhappiness.com

ISBN 978-0-9910649-7-7

First Edition

CONTENTS

I. ROMANTIC LOVE	1
II. RELATIONSHIPS	39
III. LOVE GENERALLY	77
IV. SOCIALIZATION	97
V. LOST OR UNFOUND	123
VI. MIND	163
VII. BEAUTY	179
VIII. ART	197

This book is dedicated

to

those who

love knowledge

and knowing about love

I.
ROMANTIC LOVE

I. ROMANTIC LOVE

you unfurl
my curled-up edges
setting free the shape i am

quaint little valley
among rolling hills
green clouds of trees
cut out cotton candy sky
and you

Romantic love is coincidence. It
cannot be planned or forced and may
subside as it arrived or change into
something else. This makes us afraid.

the candle melted
in the sun
some things are better reserved
for the night

you smell good
she whispered
nose tickling my neck

she learned to trust me
with her life
as i took her across
the treacherous wasteland
while she was my only hope

I. ROMANTIC LOVE

there is no mercy
in romantic love
or its absence

butterfly shells
tanning sand
give me your hand
and we shall walk

hardly anything
more attractive
than a woman's glance
over her shoulder
as she walks away

romantic love

a good anesthetic

for the tyranny of mate selection

our gazes met

my existence tore in two

one part with me and one with you

ever in need to be mended

we both touched

our screens feeling

each other's hands

by haptic transfer

only a beginning

I. ROMANTIC LOVE

i did not see

how deeply i had already fallen

my heart blinded me

knowing i would not let it happen

the sun rises

when your eyes open

and it will set when they close

separated by

a dimensional membrane

they would never join

still they could sense

the other and desire

not being there
with you
death by the seconds

she was unsure
about his feelings
and wished they would matter
to hers

when i asked
why me
she asked the same
no reason fine by us
in case it would dissolve

I. ROMANTIC LOVE

the sound of her yes
like a burning fuse
made him forget
the question

her and her horse's manes
streamed by the wind
she proudly strode
toward me on my path
only her eyes
gave the slightest hint
she was in love

Would he have hurt less without her?

for you i lay my armor down
to meet you
on the field of passion

lying with him on moss
laced with fern
she listened what nature said
rain whispering in her living leaves
and tapping on the dead

she was the tall
lonely beauty
frightening boys
at the dance

I. ROMANTIC LOVE

if i confessed
she moves me
would she come my way

let us walk in castle gardens
reminisce under towering trees
you kiss me
past my unshaven stubbles
i ask your hand
getting down on my knees

touch stopping short
of the surface
a play with yearning

i love parts of her
she does not play

Passing me toward the hot tub, she said, hardly turning: "You want it on?" "Pardon me?" She spun around, eyes rolling: "The bubble machine!"

interlocking pheromone signatures

i knew we were together
when we let silence speak

I. ROMANTIC LOVE

we want to see

the fight of a hawk

in the eyes of our loves

not the docile ogle of cattle

we want them ready

to go to extremes

upon passion's call to battle

they said we were too young

to know love

when they seemed to have forgotten

they fell toward each other

tripping over shared words

you are warm summer rain
illuminated by sunshine
drenching me

she fought him
like a lioness
half serious
and half in jest
he stayed around
he passed the test

she looked for a man
who would lock on her gaze
until she lowered her eyes

I. ROMANTIC LOVE

she asked me to meet her

after the play

in a church yard

by the theater

her ghostly appearance

in the dark

made me wonder

if i should fear her

i could not

make a rhyme

of our love

words are a poor way

to express what hearts say

they hear best beating

next to each other

the man on the train
she had not met
asking for her name
one glance in his eyes
her defiance was wrecked
she would never be the same

love divined
we dared not speak
electrifying glances

home anywhere
even the open road
except where you are not

I. ROMANTIC LOVE

on our first date
she asked me
to turn around
while she was
getting dressed

long hair skirting softly
the small of her back
resembling an untensioned bow

she dressed like a boy
while growing up
now she's wearing
my shirts in the morning

after the garden party
tables clearing band left
few chinese lanterns
still flickered
we lost our shoes
danced in the grass
to our music

he had been told
that love is patient
so he waited doting
for it to grow
then he learned
it can be passion
quickly determining
yes or no

I. ROMANTIC LOVE

slight animations
of her face
tell me about her heart

imagined her love
cupped in both hands
splashing my soul with vigor

i did not hear from her today
advancing hours withered aching
what could have taken her away
is she ok
and our love
i wonder waking

no question from when
i first looked in her eyes
how our encounter would end

annoyed by his staring
she drew a wide-eyed
open-mouthed grimace
he pulled his face
to look even crazier
that's how she fell in love

earning the trust
of a wild animal
what courting love is like

I. ROMANTIC LOVE

last time i counted
she had four dimples
but then i got lost

their hideaway was
a forest meadow
they lay on soft grass
in a cherry tree's shadow
not knowing that this
would end so soon

you excite
and settle me
at once

ultimate wildness

ultimate calm

both i experience with you

your heart is like a flower

innocently showing its petals

making everybody smile

looking out

into dark rolling waves

sitting side by side

they were preparing

their first embrace

pulling them like the tide

I. ROMANTIC LOVE

showing love
in little silly ways
the rest's too scary yet

your eyes and lips
make me surrender
yet i'm stronger than before

he could not sleep
could not breathe
could not eat
as if his life force
had left him
to be with her

every time i see her
my heart stops
to capture the moment

and then we broke
the barrier of talking
with a close-eyed kiss

people first think
they are fools for loving
for hoping their angel
would love them back
until it happens
then all makes sense

I. ROMANTIC LOVE

he looks at her achingly

afraid of attention

doubtful she likes him

or would give him a chance

she left

without goodbye

for paris

he followed

missing her

everywhere

the search

ended when

he met clarisse

with cassis lips

and raven hair

she dared him
to scale her impervious walls
wishing he would find a door

love is a game
of rising gestures and responses
leveling
or burning through earth and sky
testing whether
we can read and please the other

my memory of her
she kissed the flowers
with her eyes closed

I. ROMANTIC LOVE

what can i tell you
about my life
when it only began with you

she challenged her suitors
to state what they wanted
until one simply said you

your dad told me to leave
your brothers taunted me
your mother brought tea
neighbors are gawking
as i sit here in the rain
till you know how sorry i am again

when i see her
my soul wants to drop to the floor
for fear of having high hopes

her existence pulled on
every nerve
throughout his body
longing to experience her

what is it that makes me
find every detail of you
perfect
did i carry your image
before i ever met you

I. ROMANTIC LOVE

we drove to reach
a lonely beach
and lost us
until we found

the gold-braided girl
had ten names for her dog
and didn't carry a leash
so i asked her out

when i think of that time
what do i most miss
it's your blushing smile
and our first kiss

she was a priestess
of the forest
he bathed in her springs
of cerulean eyes
and recognized
she was not horrid
evil envy had spread such lies

my love for you
is acting cool
though it is burning me
inside
am i a fool
not letting you know
don't want to scare you
that's why i hide

I. ROMANTIC LOVE

he still was asking himself

why did she speak

to him

when he had given no reason

other than waiting

among many

and why did that paralyze him

the sudden attention

by this angelic being

to him

filthy from sleeping outside

felt like

an attack

a sick joke

a dare by her friends

he immediately assumed
something was wrong
with her
to address a man
like him
he would protect himself
by showing her
how undeserving he was

waves atomizing the beach
propounding nothing matters
except what we have right now

The cruelty of taking love for granted.

I. ROMANTIC LOVE

the girl who
did not like me
because i made her fall
in love

kissing you felt like
all falling away
leaving us
tumbling in flight

he fell for her when
she got on her knees
to worship
the tiniest blossom

watching him
tending to his guitar
she wanted
to be his music

despite hooded winter coat
gloves rubber boots
he could imagine her
underneath

she makes my heart break
open
at the fault lines
of long-paved-over dreams

I. ROMANTIC LOVE

i get lost

and found

in her

if you think she's beautiful

if you love her ways

if you respect her

if she moves you

tell her

and even more

show her

unmistakably

Not loving her is not an option.

her special
attributes
defy definition

the only way
he knew to be strong
was cold and silent
how then
could he let her in
teach me he said

a knight
in shining car more
than a valet of doors

II.
RELATIONSHIPS

II. RELATIONSHIPS

Romantic scene. She gazes at the clear, starlit night and sighs: "Isn't it perfect?" He: "Almost, if it weren't for all those little dots."

she was my opposite
like we were cast
from one another

having her in my hands
entirely and with abandon
made me nervous
i felt i could so easily break
her filigree soul

we clenched each other's hand
during the flight turbulence
and knew then we would not let go

successful relationships
persist in a mixture
of approval and acceptance

he never tired
looking at her
despite having memorized her
at any scale
recall wounded him
unless she was there

II. RELATIONSHIPS

you want to be
beautiful ever
in my heart
you always will

concurrently or alternately
we hate and love being tied down
freedom and security compete

your word smooths my waves
your touch calms my storms
your being heals my heart
or the opposite
godlike

sphere of my being
opened for you
incomplete and vulnerable

i'll never give up on you
unless you want me to
and even if you should part
i'd pine for you in my heart

half worlds apart
one was sleeping
while the other waked
one was dreaming
while the other ached

II. RELATIONSHIPS

know your lover's
favo(u)rite colo(u)rs
paint your house and yard with them

swayed by the
promise of his kisses
she stayed

i was not lost
you did not find me
love has no cost
you cannot bind me
i'm here for you now
don't ask for a vow

giving ourselves
implies obligation
of returning the gift
and two's desolation
let's stay who we are
and love from afar

he came back
she said
like that was an excuse

we hold each other
as we try to give birth
to ourselves every day

II. RELATIONSHIPS

the warmth of a fire
we both sustain
keeping our distance
for fear of the flame

i am telling you now
he said
as if timing was a formality

don't know anymore
where you start and i end
but do know for sure
what you meant
when you said we

love shows itself
clearest in the morning

she makes me forget my principles
of remaining whole and individual
meeting in the middle
being able to retreat
without catastrophic loss
theory cannot prepare
for the practice of love

in heaven's judgment
or wrath of hell
i will hold your hand

II. RELATIONSHIPS

When I was little, I trusted The Beatles for years when they sang "Eight Days A Week" until I finally counted and found they had lied to me. I also took away from the lyrics that loving a girl is never complete and that you don't get time off. They weren't lying about that.

She just wanted to be safe.

all others left
she stayed
though i had told her to go

if we believe
ever having anyone
we have been had

i never asked you to love me
he said
as if it would have made a difference

i will not
let put hold you down
want to see you soar
in heavens of light
and free to join me more
in our common flight

II. RELATIONSHIPS

so here's the deal
she proclaimed
as her unconditional love
entered negotiations

how do i know in the dark
you are and will be there
i feel an enduring arc
lighting my heart with your care

a cavern lit with love
while outside storms are raging
a period filled with present
while other concerns are aging

yes yes she said

a little too fast

he wanted her to mean it

standing

at the edge of our ocean

will it rip us apart in a burst

will it drown us

or will it leave us stranded

or endlessly dying of thirst

reality

never caught up

to my dreams of us

II. RELATIONSHIPS

don't ask me
to be fully yours
unless you are fully mine

the more i have you
the more i want you
the more i give my all
to be worthy of your trust

he her
opener of jars
fixer of all broken
listener holder carrier rest
would falter without her

i love you
for loving all
needing love

it's a mistake
i cannot mend
she's already read the rhyme
but i will go forward in time
write a more loving end
for both our sake

do we leave
for our love
or stand up for a change

II. RELATIONSHIPS

not being able to live
without someone
fuses elation and horror

telling me you love me
is like describing food

ice windows
we broke open in ruts
left right
while we talked
when she took my hand
in her coat pocket saying
let's just walk

i know you think
i don't love you enough
but i love you so much it hurts
sometimes i just cannot stand it

you mind me
uncaring
whether i'm worthy
of your attention

let's just drive
he said so far
we won't remember
and fall in love all over

II. RELATIONSHIPS

i want to know

your truth

and feel it

and want to

let you in

on mine

so we can have

a life together

where darkness yields

to the light we shine

it was fall

our fall

thank the winter

for freezing it all

so now we can rise again

she did not like him
in the mornings
seeing her spent
leaving the seat up
wanting breakfast
trying to hold her
on her way out

when she asked
do you love me still
he knew it had all gone wrong

while he held her
she stopped living

II. RELATIONSHIPS

she trusts me enough
not to hide her flaws

women are flowers
men are bees

i did not change
inside me
what you see
was always there
knowing me better
will you stay with me
or leave me
asunder from your care

he was given
to cloudbursts
due to her shun

the proof of his love
began in earnest
when hers ended

he kissed off her tears
one by one
dissolving her pain to peace
he had no idea
what he had done
an insufficient ease

II. RELATIONSHIPS

Women don't necessarily prefer bad boys, but they want a mate with character, not a doormat for them or anybody else.

he deeply loves her
for her body
but when it fades
where will his love be

holding on
to each other in the currents
are we making it harder
to keep our heads above water

crisp fall air reborn
old university life
and lectures
from my new girlfriend

holding you
but you hold me
when your love
infuses me

he knew that without her
not much else would matter
why did it feel different
within her love

II. RELATIONSHIPS

i want to walk with you forever
between the tides
of life's coast line

did she leave for good
or to see
whether he would follow
or if she wanted to return
he had to find out
at the risk of
ruining last chances

when the initial rush wears off
lovers turn to other questions

she chided him
predictable
until she needed that

she said
she had not been
looking for me
and finding me
ended her dreams

as long as i can be
free with you
i don't mind
never being free of you

II. RELATIONSHIPS

she took the worries

out of my life

by filling it with nows

afraid of events

coming to a head

she kept her composure

until decomposure

regardless

of what this world is

or where we are

we can be certain

we are together

marriage is scary
because it seals love
into a compromising position

not that she did not care anymore
but she had to care for herself

i never want to feel
i missed living
my love for you

I can, you fizz, we pop.

II. RELATIONSHIPS

she kept dancing

after we met

i tried not to break her stride

her love

a maelstrom

of rose petals

the softest bed

when she settled down

his love

a shelter

built from strong hands

opening to let her bloom

she came to him
without hesitation
would she leave
in a similar way

she did not steal
was just safekeeping
his heart
so he would not leave

volcanic tornado
when he hurt her
same in a good way
when he didn't

II. RELATIONSHIPS

Sometimes she just wants to be
held like a child.

the kind of girl
who would beat him at sports
then claim he let it happen

she said her body would be a gift
that could not be returned

If we had not met, would we be in
love with someone else?

ocean flags warning
waves springing high
we ride them gently
until they die

casually saying
i'll play you a song
he hoped she was ready
for his message

father friend brother boy
not only husband
mother friend sister girl
not only wife

but that's alright
she sadly concludes
as if it won't hurt her too much

the prime elixir
to love's persistence
is letting each other be

linking fates terrifies
for lost control
of our flights
we will fall
unless we learn
to move our wings together

after all this time
of hardship
her softness
still disarmed him

you say you're not
what i take you for
but i sense a glow
of long-buried embers
when you speak of your life

your head resting
on my shoulder
makes me stronger but not bolder

II. RELATIONSHIPS

she measured his love
by his coming around
after being mistreated
when he stopped her game
and found a new life
she claimed he had cheated

i could be perfectly
what she wants
as long as she wants
the real me

Contests in a relationship must have two objectives: Advancing us and us.

Men emancipate from mothers only
to become dependent again on
women they love. Female power
could change the world.

a man
pacified by a woman
is not warlike
shared responsibility

Men gear many of their actions to
win women's favor or to distract from
their despair of lacking acceptance.
Much can be learned from this.

II. RELATIONSHIPS

Men have screwed up our world, but women have let them. Not asserting their power has permitted imbalance.

Humanity needs women to assert themselves and take responsibility as women, not as imitators of men.

Women are diminished in some cultures due to a fearful insight that their power could rein in men's natural penchants for violence and domination. But women may be complicit in valuing these traits.

oppression of women
results from
amorality of men
and women's collusion

Gender blindness is not the solution
but part of gender discrimination.
Humans have a fundamental right to
respect, including their gender.

tired of keeping
the home together
while men go out
visiting pain on the world

III.
LOVE
GENERALLY

III. LOVE GENERALLY 79

love is a haven
not a finishing school
desire for harmony
must come from within

Calling dedication to something a
passion is notable because the
expressed willingness to suffer does
not portray constructive expectations.

true love may be spent
until we resent
but never does
entirely end

Love is thorny because it makes us want to possess in mutuality what possesses us. Yet the odds seem overwhelming that objects of our love will not adequately reciprocate.

Caveat amator. Love is an irrational mixture of "becauses" and "no-matter-whats" exposing us to risks of misjudgment and abuse.

if love is returned
its offer of sacrifice
will be rejected

III. LOVE GENERALLY 81

hands we don't lend
hearts we won't mend
soon we will die
no one will cry
is this how we want to end

Some use love, even in its painful aspects, as a drug to distract from other concerns in their life.

Are those fixated on loving and being loved by higher beings compromising the natural need of humans to love and be loved by one another?

before you left you said
you would try to send me
a sign
of your forever true love
you already did at that time

love wants to please
criticism
an accusation
of its absence

persnickety hearts
misers of love
shriveled before death

III. LOVE GENERALLY

if you would not give up everything

except love

it's not true love

if you would not ask for anything

except love

it's not true love

love pulls us up

from pain's surrender

last line of defense

love

renewing hope

that entrusted life will be tended

all our life we yearn
get used to fulfillment
and yearn for something else
love can survive then only
by never being taken for granted

for someone unfamiliar
with love
it feels like an imposition

mind what you say
to those who love you
their heart takes you
at your every word

III. LOVE GENERALLY

to be loved

frightens us

if we doubt us worthy

of such a commitment

it cannot last

categories of love

romantic

for family and friends

humanity

other life

nature and its provenance

different

but matching pieces

of one theme

requiring overall integration

not hating
leaves room
for love in our heart

Even if science could explain love or
any other emotion and lay open its
mechanisms, its sensations would
remain immediately mysterious to us.

when people you love
make mistakes
be kind
or they might decide
you were one

III. LOVE GENERALLY

love coarsely declined
breeds hate
an easily prevented ill

romantic love
demands one object
other varieties should be more open

We must feel compassion with everything to create the conditions for universal peace. Yet the resulting pain would be intolerable without the healing aspects of love, including forgiveness, inspiration, and trust.

If we should forget all we ever learned, we still would possess the most valuable knowledge from which and with which we were born: Love.

Sustaining love requires continual renewal. One-sided love suffers and may deplete from lack of return. Yet reciprocity creates unlimited energy.

watching you sleep
i will protect you
watching you wake
i'll clear the clouds

III. LOVE GENERALLY

loving the world

pulls us in pain

the ways it is injured

could drive us insane

but love it we must

for our salvation

and prospects

of even greater elation

the tenderest force

is also the strongest

When we love, we can sense

intuitively that all is vibration.

reasons

for loving

backups for our heart

thinking why we love

is a fruitless exercise

compassion forgiveness

inspiration and trust

do not license evil

they look beyond

to peaceful harmony

and equip us to get there

in the most succinct way

III. LOVE GENERALLY

take a day
for what and whom you love
then try to make it a habit

Not loving people as they are wounds
them because we love someone else
instead who does not exist.

we must love people
as they are
love's not a reward for complying
it is enlightenment
for every heart
meant to send spirits flying

peace is simple
when we stop thinking
of love as a weakness

love's affinity is cooperation
hate's affinity is competition

his innocence was that
he loved the world
and had no fear
he was called naive
deemed a threat
or hailed for his courage
he only claimed to be finally human

III. LOVE GENERALLY

humanity steeped
in senseless anguish
for nothing has value
without love

true love speaks clearly
it does not leave doubts
it does not have pride
it does not play games

people tell me
i care too much
but i don't care
what they say

love metered
give and take
just let it out

The only real threat of death is that it ends our ability to love.

Let us describe a world governed by love and then build it.

I cannot figure why feeling love is not recognized as a sense.

III. LOVE GENERALLY

driven equally
by love and fear
of not being loved

Love teaches our rational mind the essence of life.

For love impossibility does not exist.

when evil and brash
demand attention
let love and gentleness shine

the enemy traits of love are many
counter them and be redeemed

home
a big heart pumping
life through its chambers

Imagine your life without each person
in it and tell those you would miss.

Life is a lover challenging us to
declare what we really want.

IV.
SOCIALIZATION

IV. SOCIALIZATION

Socialization is a fundamental need of humans that encompasses several subcategories requiring human interaction. Additionally, we have a fundamental need to be in and interact with nature. Deprivation of either will cause deep unhappiness. Consideration of these facts can point us to establishing and abiding by wholesome terms of conduct.

Social interactions are essential for human wellbeing in multiple aspects. Individuals therefore have the right to situate themselves in ways that optimize such interactions for them.

Socialization requires common or at least commonly accepted objectives and means. Social needs and fears of social incoherence may engender arrangements enhancing happiness. However, they may also cement benefits at less than optimal levels or lead societies fundamentally astray.

Socialization is a selfish undertaking with essential ulterior effects. It creates value for counterparts of socialization efforts to obtain return benefits. Yet some needs guiding socialization derive direct satisfaction from ulterior improvements.

IV. SOCIALIZATION

People build walls around them so they won't get hurt only to discover they made themselves prisoners.

It was an age when people wondered what scheme someone being nice to them attempted pulling to take advantage of them, or they suspected weakness currying their favor.

You will never be more alone than when everybody thinks you have many reasons to be happy, but you are not as happy as you should be.

she tried to shield her heart
by rigid hair
marked face
mirrored sunglasses
plated jewelry
loud clothes
violent shoes
defensive smoking

darkness like a blanket
to ward the warmth within

others might not care for you
unless you care for others

IV. SOCIALIZATION

when people say
they want to help
and then they actually do

he did not allow
himself to love
anything living
because he feared
not being able
to stand its loss

he was in love with
his reflection by her
and her reflection on him

if we care only for ourselves
all that is not us
is consumable infringing
or uninteresting
a reduced way to live

why could we not live
our whole life on the beach
because land people
would not let us

sometimes we have nothing
hoping to find the reset button
we will discover it in solitude

IV. SOCIALIZATION

an ocean of islands

and bobbing bottles

with paper wrapped snippets

of brains and hearts

we click in cells

compose messages

commit them to the ether

in hopes to be found

rush hour pedestrians

flooding past him

stunned cold

expressions of swarming fish

ignoring those in trouble
should offend us endlessly
but we are doing well

we may want to
insulate ourselves
in capsules
of love and good will
from a sea of ugliness
but how can we hope
it will carry us

If they do not already care somehow,
chances are they never will.

IV. SOCIALIZATION

singing boldly to break the silence

and seeking warmth

in the cold of the night

they felled the proud tree

he had planted as child

and called him a sissy for crying

most humans

won't break down

if nobody's there

to catch them

windfall of indifference

orderly desperation

we talk a nice game
but in the end
walk on by
things to do
no one's helping us either

Pray you never go down. People you
know will ignore your plight, tread
and prey upon you, making living
with them difficult after you recover.

family, friends, acquaintances
may drop us
if we don't lift them

IV. SOCIALIZATION

People react to us largely acting out
their settings, particularly if they
do not know or care about us.

numbing neglect
or courting dance
the utility of people

some say
she is out of her mind
for thinking too much of others
irked she shows
humankind to be kind
in a world where nobody bothers

humanity is reeling
from kind words never said
and kind deeds never done

who will help
when we fall
reality not felt
while walking tall

not one got here undamaged
but we healed and prepared
with one another's help
to spread our wings
and give our spirits flight

IV. SOCIALIZATION

isolation

sentence

for the crime of being different

a call for help

let it go to voice mail

and say i never got the message

innocent trust

of babies' eyes

we were once like this

now we must conquer

evil's rise

returning to that bliss

closed doors had burned
into the screen of his life
mirages of openings

In the end, the friendship we give and
receive matters most.

this morn i found
a tiny winged person
curled up
in a blanket left outside
she asked me to tell you
not to worry
everything will be alright

IV. SOCIALIZATION

this human's marked
to be discarded
go wish the best of luck

we hope the doomed
will be keeping quiet and
refrain from spoiling our delight

Ask nothing, trust to give.

The world would be friendlier
if we befriended new people.

We may suffer needlessly because we are too proud to admit helplessness or ask for help. Assistance is a human trait, but we may have to activate it.

What a great world it can be if we help one another. We can witness the power of love unfold and envelop us. Why are we not acting accordingly?

Good human relations are simple on any level. We all could be friends if we would practice what we should learn in early childhood.

IV. SOCIALIZATION

Much would be achieved if we would approach one another as respectful, compassionate friends even if we do not agree with or know the other.

Care. The world is a desperate place much more through carelessness than intentional malice, which is also frequently caused by carelessness.

voice to the voiceless
healing to the hurt
progressions of kindness
may start with a word

Friends stand with us so we might
stand with them or what they value.

surround yourself
with people to embrace
in joy anxiety and grief

i did not come here for advice
just to hear myself and reflect
thanks for helping me listen

True friendship survives any trouble.

IV. SOCIALIZATION

We can find our humanity by
considering other individuals
alternate versions of ourselves.

Knowing the power of friendship,
we also know weakness and dread
when it is absent.

free abandon
cut flower
forgiving its killing
to be adored
cheering the day
reminding us in the end

so much separating us
so different we are
that is why we need one another
minding our commonalities

he called me friend
and said it's a short fall
to sleeping on the sidewalk

between hiding shy
and want for notice
she is hard to figure out
thinking she's ugly and awkward
her soul wants to scream out loud

IV. SOCIALIZATION

i'll be there when you need me
reserved for best friends
why are we so ungenerous

merciless daytime glare
on agony uncovered
made her blend into darkness
and neon lights
to cool the hot pitch
of her burning soul

the fight
to prove love
may stunt it

the girl
who hung out
with the older boys
protected by them
when they played
caring for them
in their final years
kindness and kindness repaid

berlin once proud
for the wrong reasons
like so many capitals
not anymore
rising from defeat
to search for honesty
a lesson others have yet to learn

IV. SOCIALIZATION

a random network

of hands reaching out

together we can heal the earth

no soul can claim

to be alone

if it is not

the only one

searching

following callings

will lose you false friends

begrudging your

moving ahead

insisting on attributions of fault
instead of fostering healing
scoring bringing good will to a halt
raising continued ill feeling

grace is
making everybody feel important
including yourself

preoccupied with having their way
uncaring or hostile
unless they need someone
the inconsiderately selfish
destroy faith in humankind

V.
LOST
OR
UNFOUND

V. LOST OR UNFOUND

look

she said

avoiding my eyes

head resting muscles tensed

she felt like a baby deer

torn between the warmth

and ensnarement

of unfamiliar human embrace

so he set her free

i was there

waiting

we lost a great time

too much has happened
to start anew
no more of the trust
i once had in you

all had failed
quietly gazed
calmly walked
not turning around
toward the chance of love to be found

you opened all doors of my heart
now icy winds are blowing through
nobody's home

V. LOST OR UNFOUND

i will always remember you
he said signaling
she was dead to him

lost love calls for surgery
to live with yourself again
but after unsuccessful trials
you settle for its demotion

she cries
i could have saved him
mourning being alive
still contortions for giving in
seem greater sacrifice

oh no not we
we were bulletproof
until we let it happen

could say goodbye
a million times
it would not change a thing

millions of waves
have curled on by
and i surfed quite a few
then you had me crashing
from way up high
still don't know what to do

V. LOST OR UNFOUND

traveling different circles now
sidestepping when they cross
recalling they lost direction somehow
establishing who was boss

falling in love
i devoted my senses
solely to feeling her
she left me in utter deprivation
devoid of myself and care

can't thank you enough
for your goodbye
i met her moving on

the weight of lone love
was crushing him
until she let him go
now days are gray
and his light is dim
but slowly rekindling its glow

sick of love with her
then and now she's gone
wish there were an antidote

she said seven
at the old bridge tower
but she never came

V. LOST OR UNFOUND

i had her as much
as one can have another
but did not know
what that meant

refusing acceptance
she had a new life
he told everybody she died

thinking it sounded devout
he claimed to love her for her soul
as if her body was without
a part less worthy than the other
his pious demeanor became a bother

how do you say
goodbye
to someone
who's already left

not a word
not a look
not a touch
it's senseless

waiting for a better train
or deeming herself a destination
she missed her connection
and now lives at the station

V. LOST OR UNFOUND

she left him claiming
he was wanting
she left him wanting
to claim her

high in years
she confided in me
she had spurned
the love of her life
he had foretold
how contrite she would be
when she departed in strife

You had me at goodbye.

it crossed her mind
to cross the sea
this crossed a line
he crossed her plan
but crossed his heart
when she got cross
a cross he has to bear

go home she said
as if i still had one
apart from her

reversed love
the coldest frost

V. LOST OR UNFOUND

bristling distance

are you ok

he should not have asked her

into the cafe

now that she was just crying

fighting for someone

to love you

is senseless

love happens

or not

when you

show yourself

but that

you must do

to find love

she fervently asked
why don't you love me
he was ashamed
not having an answer

don't cry
how you loved her
but didn't dare show
true love would have found a way

shallow affinities may end
but deeper love does not
even enmity and hate
can't let it completely rot

V. LOST OR UNFOUND

she resisted admitting
it was over
pretending her fear of him
was love

all he wanted now
was to forget her
and even forget
that he forgot

upon losing her
he kept tiredly roaming
searching to fill
the void in his being

crushed roses
honesty too soon
you should have
let them wither

you've kept silent
all this time
while i left something
that was mine
my hope i need it back

apricot skin and flesh
her core poisonous as well
he had to have all of her still

V. LOST OR UNFOUND

now he's on
to his second wife
because she is not
what he made his first

he watched sports
until his life ended
she's taking classes
to forget

heading toward golf
with her bowl-bellied husband
secretly wished she could go
with the runners

i thought
you were reaching
to touch my heart
but you kept walking
right through

An unnerving prospect of falling in love is that we will carry the person affecting us so deeply in our heart for a lifetime, even if our feelings change.

not being able to be with
or without someone
five purgatories of love

V. LOST OR UNFOUND

The most brutal feature of nature's programming is falling in love and not being caught in the arms of the other, not even to break the fall.

sweetness
she stuck to me
during the night
in daylight she denied

i opened a door
to her demons
she slammed it close
to protect me or them

silent girl

jailed in herself

wishing she could escape

he tried to reach her

to set her free

defenses

kept shutting her gate

she wanted to burn them

though he was gone

his love letters still seemed alive

i had only love for her

she said it wasn't enough

V. LOST OR UNFOUND

many flee into love
as a refuge from
a loveless world
how sad
and what a burden

don't hold my hand
she snipped as we walked
i'm certainly not blind

i remember
phone numbers of women
whose names and features
i long forgot

approaching the ferry
lone stretch of highway
grass waving golden
late afternoon heat
couple in sports car
tearing past me
could not help wishing
to be in his seat

he did his best
to refute affection
for fear of obligation

Fate made alternate arrangements.

V. LOST OR UNFOUND

i once knew a girl
who should have been you
saving me
lots of grief

going where we
were with lovers
deathly haunting
of ourselves

chestnut flower and lilac scent
lay heavy on evening air
i walked alone the path we went
heard people laughing somewhere

lonely fenced gardens
dogs barking at me
in familiar language

i've missed you
since we failed to meet
but in my dreams we're joined

he tended her
waiting for her
to thrive and open
ignoring
she had been
cut and dried

V. LOST OR UNFOUND

rows of lit windows
to warm better worlds
i walk cold streets
as long as it hurts

really
she said
when he told her
he loved her
it was all for naught

he held on to the pain
of losing her
the last feeling about her he had

i was not there
when all else was
regrets
i could not see

once she flooded
his every sense
his hope finally died
when she left
his dreams

he imagines her presence
every spring when peonies
open to dew-filled breezes

V. LOST OR UNFOUND

her kiss set my world on fire
for her it was more
like kicking a tire

staying away from her
after confessing his love
nearly killed him
he knew he had to though
if this was ever to be

please
she implored him
please
he brushed her off

she did not want him
headed for war
he shot two kids
who did not stop their car
she called him her hero
being back
as if his heart
had not thrice broken yet

the loneliest place is
where he used to live

she did not open her door anymore
for resenting the sound of the bell

V. LOST OR UNFOUND

the hardest trial in life
is living without someone
one cannot live without

opening window
train leaving station
another caught up
track next to mine
a girl held a hand out
we touched for a moment
i asked how are you
she smiled and said fine

touch rarest form of communication

filled with love
that no one wanted
she had to kill it to survive

her sweetness
was frosting
on cold ambition
his cool demeanor
a shield
over tremors

relinquishing integrity
demanding reciprocity
banes of romantic love

V. LOST OR UNFOUND

how could it be
you held out for me
to ruin someone's life

we could have been friends
had she let me down easy
but she did not care for my heart

she claims no recall
to mask the pain
of trying to forget
what must have happened
no one knows
she's keeping it like that

grateful

you filled

my heart with love

sorry

its burning to ashes

left you cold

hopeful

i rose today

to move on

i carried a poem

that perfectly reflected

my feelings and thoughts

about you and me

but searching for it lately

i cannot find it anymore

V. LOST OR UNFOUND

finally ready
confessing my love
she's ready for moving on

this time was different
they could not return

she asked me threateningly
not to love you
now we're not married anymore

She sometimes tried to imagine love.

your love will never satisfy me
to where i want to settle down
my demons send me
down the highway
to try my luck in some other town

he pushed
and pulled
until she left
so he could declare
he kept holding on

if i could touch her world
would her bubble burst

V. LOST OR UNFOUND

unhappy and lost

she thought

judging and dismissing

would find her what she wanted

yet for this reason

what she wanted

continued to escape

she was not hearing

frantically tearing

voices screaming

in her head

he was repeating

how much he loved her

she responded

i wish i were dead

if you let a lover go
be merciful
gently crush all their hopes

lacking courage
to follow her heart
scanning for defects
until she finds them
no prince appears
she sleeps hundred years

a couple eating silently
because everything
has been said

V. LOST OR UNFOUND

the feeling went away
she knew not what to say
he tried to make her stay
but had lost all sway

senses head and heart
all signal matches
for positive imaginations
how will we handle disappointment

loathing her heart for hanging on
steadfastly through the pain
knowing all hope has long been gone
thinking she must be insane

they keep telling her
to forget him
that she must start a new life
when all her cells hold a secret code
avowing her oath as his wife

sense of a dog finding mate or master
butterfly's grit migrating the earth
sailor tied to a mast in disaster
she did not give up
until giving birth

why does holding you lately
feel like embracing myself

V. LOST OR UNFOUND

she says she
was not ready then
but i am not ready now

she wanted to love him
and gave it some time
while truth was staring her down

hard rain falling
cleansing nature
she wished she could
cast off the roof
and open her body
to wash all of him away

no use
for this circus
she'll never perceive you
you're not the attraction
she's looking for

avoiding her
as a reminder
of his failings

he had to let go
since she never responded
but maybe something prevented her
hope's lie to despairing existence

VI.
MIND

VI. MIND

every heart carries a fire
to light warm spark
or burn dim and die

That rational thought is motivated by emotions has been woefully ignored or dismissed in philosophy, other sciences, and common life.

Betterment is often foreclosed because people do not want to alter their ways. Much pain may have to occur for them to change their minds and take corrective action.

we must show our mind
regardless of odds
and risks of being burned
we may not rise from
the mock of false dreams
if truth is never learned

love unlocks hearts
allowing minds
different perspectives

we must relinquish pride
and admit reality
to engender positive change

VI. MIND

Many people carry thick shells. Little gets in or out. How isolated and lonely they must be. How frustrating for others to get through to them.

Follow your heart, they say, as if we could do anything else. Yet we must harmonize the multiple emotions that rule our heart before we act.

they laughed when he sang
danced or played make-believe
tasking his life
with unfreezing his heart

perceptions thoughts emotions

are given to us

as inconclusive fragments

it is up to us

to sort and purify them

put them together

and find what is missing

grief drenched earth

from human abuses

pollution of our hearts

Our mind oscillates between wanting

and possessing. Then time is up.

VI. MIND

all we express mindfully

is to convince someone

maybe ourselves

standing up words like soldiers

close not your skull

nor lock your heart

lest you be lost

scaffolds and ladders of my mind

trodden loose and swaying

in meandering consciousness

will i ever know their purpose

or are they the entire construct

many are too dulled or frenzied
for exploring and reflecting
responsibility of external forces
or willing authorization

In helping others to set their mind
free, we must be careful not to
impose our ideas or induce chaos. An
orderly process appears advisable.

Much frustration or other pain arises
because, caught up in our mind, we
tend to overestimate how similar
others are or should be to us.

VI. MIND

It is astounding what we can learn by listening and observing before speaking and how this can improve our mind, communications, and resulting activities.

time flies
for absent minds
a lesser problem for children

We expend much time and effort creating settings in our mind and externalities to simulate a higher state of being than we hold.

Future years will silently reverberate with our hopes and aspirations, none knowing we lived there in our mind unless we can bridge the gap.

seeing through optics
of preconceptions
tuning into reality
requires mental adjustments

Much is revealed or can be obtained by opening our minds. Closed minds create the most obstructive and destructive force humanity faces.

VI. MIND

"All I want is . . . ." Finish the sentence, and you express a limit set in your mind. Is there nothing left to do after you have reached it?

Mindfulness is a concept better called mindlessness. It may have a place. Yet we eventually must turn to arrange existential objectives and pursuits.

Ask yourself: Am I fully using my physical, perceptive, emotional, and intellectual potential? If the answer is "no" or "I don't know," ask why.

our mind is cut in facets of

senses and imaginations

rationality and emotion

knowledge and speculation

reality and dreams

conscious and subconscious

prose and poetry

The danger of making up our mind is
that it will be made up.

having found precise ways
to state rational concepts
we still struggle conveying our hearts

VI. MIND

some people have us
pegged in a second
expecting us to work hard
if we want to change their minds

Are we not mere observers of our perceptions, thoughts, and emotions, registering ourselves as machines that are familiar yet strangely obscure?

Lazy persons may not have suffered a trauma or lack of care to make them so. They may naturally not be set for high ambition levels or their pursuit.

We are daily amnesiacs of intricate
stories that move us profoundly at
night, leaving us with faint ghosts of
ourselves during waking hours.

surely a computer
can win a chess match
but why would it
want to play

conscious on the surface
like a lake fed by
a deep unexplored cavern
underneath

VI. MIND

perception reproduces reality
emotion spurs design
thought yields mechanics
action creates new reality
the cycle starts again

Life would be easier if we shared our perceptions, emotions, and thoughts instead of hiding or falsifying them, or trouncing one another with them.

Rational thought does not give us reasons to live or live happily. The sources lie in our emotions.

the seed of a concept
grown and matured by consideration
into deliberate action
or swallowed by instinctive shortcut

reason is an instrument
employed by needs

Detailed awareness of how emotions and rational processes work may one day allow us their intricate control. However, exercising such control will keep requiring their overall assessment and harmonization.

VII.
BEAUTY

VII. BEAUTY

The greatest pain for the unwise is beauty they cannot possess. Act with respect and decency, then beauty will rise in you and join you.

    the feeling
    of good shoes
    goes to her head

    some beauty will pass
    like a day
    leaving
    what we feel
    when night comes

beauty has supreme power
empires are built and destroyed
in seeking to possess it

can't stand
too much beauty
without possession
to soothe the ugly
inside of us

Captivating beauty awes us and fills us with wonder. But to inspire deeper and lasting attachment, it must tell its story and permit our connection.

VII. BEAUTY

beauty

inspiration

and vehicle

for another try

to approach pleasure

Beauty may be hard to bear when it stirs pain in us about unattained or destroyed beauty. But keep your mind open because beauty mends.

beauty among ugliness

essential reminder

of what life should be

old couple holding hands
renews my hope
that beauty can survive
although its focus may change

you convince me
beauty can win anywhere
because it has in me through you

beauty
siren of infinite goodness
inviting us to live in her
and not mind
dying in her arms

VII. BEAUTY

Beauty can be found in the symmetry
of a snow flake, but also in the
entropy of a gnarled tree.

the most beautiful places
littered with atrocities
hate and misplaced pride
all participants deemed
themselves good guys
and their crimes justified

beauty is not a luxury
it is harmony
with the universe

beauty is an inborn principle
of the cosmos
ugliness a temporary disruption

beauty and love
defy definition
mysterious
protean
closely related
endless
they define us

Beauty reduces evil by deputizing us
to serve its harmony requirements.

VII. BEAUTY

we cannot own beauty
it will always flow
we only continue
to walk in its glow
by receiving and giving away

why is untouched by man
the greatest compliment
of beauty

the insecure and jealous
want deference and shame
from unencumbered beauty
to spread indecent pain

she bathed

in moonlight

nothing i could have added

her beauty was unconscious

until i told her

i could not help it

i see you

makeup off

hair frayed

deflated pose

you think

i love you less

VII. BEAUTY

i love the way
the rising sun
illuminates your hair

blinking a second
you smile to yourself
then share your happy place

what does she think of me
losing orientation
in her presence
stammering her name
her beauty's brightness
blinds me in my darkness

we all have beautiful potentials
but whether we are beautiful
depends on how we treat them

true beauty shines
as a light from within
as if our bodies
were lanterns

many girls may be pretty
but beautiful girls
stand apart
their aura is markedly heady
because they expose their heart

VII. BEAUTY

beautiful woman
assured admiration
but how will she know
when she's loved

seeing you
as you are
convinces me
straight lines
are greatly overrated

those suffering darkness
most beautiful souls
because they appreciate light

even her cuttings
of hair on the floor
keep echoing her beauty

the modeling agency
needed fresh blood
a vampire scheme of some sort

freed of my gravity
i fall up dimensions
to unknown realms
when i look in your eyes
please ground me gently
after these highs

VII. BEAUTY

blossoms like girls
sense the curtness of beauty
intuitive teachers
for living each day

the woman flowering
by the meadow stream
unapproachable
lest he would scare her

don't look now she said
while she was not
what she thought
he wanted her to be

a pretty woman
with ugly attitude
will have an ugly life
users will value
her bodily beauty
but only for a while

matchless accessory
of women's features
a coronet of daisies

her eyes mean
end and
endlessness to me

VII. BEAUTY

in a far forest clearing

she lies

looking up

into summer rain

wears nothing

but a ladybug earring

her skin is prickling

like champagne

beauty

pointing to time

fading possibilities

and measures to enjoy

yet also a sense of

eternity and completeness

in a moment

pretty trying to be ugly

rejecting all its potential for grace

she seemed

like nature in the morning

fresh snow

or a clearing

where shy animals graze

he felt sadness

with his hunger

natural beauty

she was his

to be natural with

VIII.
ART

VIII. ART

wayward words

of grief and beauty

like tears and kisses

thrown into the wind

still it's important i can hear them

Poetry is the most intimately and successfully reproduced art form. Most humans know and recite spoken or musically enhanced poems.

We look to poetry to make a rhyme of the world or to wonder about the absence thereof.

Philosophy and its derived sciences describe and speculate about what we can rationally comprehend. Poetry also addresses what lies beyond.

Poets attempt to reflect themselves in a code they hope kindred minds can understand. For both, knowing such understanding is like coming home.

Poetry permits expression we might not be able or dare to state or hear in prose. It may hence be one of the best media to inspire changing the world.

VIII. ART

Poetry becomes bad when you try to
impress somebody - even yourself.

Poetry is the light of reality passed
through the filters, lenses, mirrors,
and prisms of our senses, thoughts,
and emotions. A clear view is science.

in poetry
worth our attention
truth love life beauty wisdom hope
and pain of their absence
reach out to us
undisturbed by time

Poetry only gives outward symbols we each must interpret with experiences. All language functions like that. But references to emotions are subjective.

You cannot force creating poetry. It arises and reveals itself to you on its terms, or you are just knitting words.

one day soon
computers will write
poems that are
random or trite
leaving the art to humans

VIII. ART

Poetry is the language of dreams
touching tips of our waking mind.

sincere words pierce
every two-dimensional surface
reaching us in depth

dance poet
hand out free chocolates
you will change nothing

Poetry writes me.

As everything in the universe, art is frequency and amplitude. Its clarity, distortion, melody, randomness, harmony, and dissonance at various levels illustrate universal concepts.

There is not much poetry in words unless they make room for readers' imagination.

poetic words
are little hammers
fit for ringing bells in us
in hope we recognize the music

VIII. ART

Some poetry must be written and
read without too much thinking.

poets resent lost love
for taking their muse
but cherish it
for granting them another

some day all
poems may be written
music composed
depictions prepared
stories told
science unveiled and applied

in poetry like any art
our dream mind
gets to speak

materialists ridicule poets
while seeking riches
that turn to dust

he finally had enough
stumbling over
the same rocks
dug them out
tossed them in a bucket
called them poetry

VIII. ART

poetic love is truest
it reigns among those
whose souls converse

words in rhyme
ruthless competition
for harmony

Poetry does not have to meet rules or make sense, but must strike a nerve.

Poetry is emotional communication.

Trying to define art is a mostly futile exercise because art attempts to represent what cannot be defined.

Poems are little traps for consciousness to catch itself.

poetry like any art
gives imagination flight

he is gone
all his poetry now a lie

VIII. ART

Then one day they had exchanged all
distant impressions and yearnings
and decided to resolve them together.

Where my poems come from is as
inscrutable to me as where they go.

Not all rhyme is poetry.

the greatest pain about writing
is taking time out
of a life wanting to be lived

If words do not naturally flow in your mind, you can never be a great writer.

You have nothing to write unless you have something to say.

words and rhymes
like frequently used shopping bags
i should only pick meanings
i carry inside my head and heart

Art helps motivate our mind.

VIII. ART

music people like
or dislike
tells much about
their state of mind

my guitar lets me
proclaim to you
what my body and words
don't yet dare to express

Good music arises when it follows the sounds and emotions of language. Everything else is just mathematics, bombast, or empty noodling.

all my colors run and blended
into muddy blues
she is love in spectral chroma
painting coats of lively hues

Find your music within and search
for harmony beyond.

Music proves harmony is not stasis.

playing unconsciously
an out-of-body experience

VIII. ART

I love cello and guitar for their
mimicry of human voices, resonance
with the human body, tactility of
play, and likeness to a woman's back.

i want to be a composer
since as a muse i chose her
or rather she chose to be
her music composes me

it was a dark stormy night
a start that sounded too trite
chose a bright calm day instead
still nothing that would be read

art asks for states

short of fulfillment

and abhors saturation

they loved the same music

and tried to avoid it

after their dance had ended

but echoes of love

kept playing on

striking them unattended

birds have the impulse

of wanting to sing

regardless of whether we hear

VIII. ART

a sudden creak
from my guitar
it's trying to unwind

every artist's nightmare
that inspiration will stop

good art proposes honesty
to its maker and consumer

art may dispense us from being real
still shows us reality in how we feel

art is an attempt

to point to harmony

or a lack thereof

nature is not an artist

it is the model

an artist tries to emulate

or from which he tries to deviate

just like a scientist

art is a reflection

of external or internal nature

in reproduction

of actual or imagined perception

VIII. ART

Art is an attempt to bend reality to our will, if only in our mind.

Distortions of reality can point us to its essence, purpose, or possibilities.

Not knowing is not the death of art. It and the desire to know are conditions for artistic undertakings.

We call nature art when it reflects our emotions.

Exploratory parallels between art and science are considerable. To progress, both must venture into outer reaches of human grasp. But art transcends evident and speculative facts in the direction of purpose or its absence.

Owning art objects is pointless and ultimately impossible because their true value lies in their message, which can only be hidden or shared.

Each human is a complex work of art arising from self-reflective work.

VIII. ART

The two aspects of art can be both described as interests in artificiality: The emulation of natural facilities and a rise to unprecedented heights.

Initially, art flows from love and admiration for the complexities and harmonies of nature, its creation of us, and the ready support it provides.

Art also flows from humans' self-love as a desire to be free from and surpass nature, to use and determine nature instead of staying subject to its order.

Venturing into secrets of nature to capture them as our reality, take its helm, and conceive its expansions or alternate courses, we increasingly take on its identity and faculties.

As we mature, our loves for nature and ourselves are bound to merge. Our highest ideal is the harmonious joinder of artificial and natural realms representing the entirety of our love.

Art and science characterize the constructive essence of humanity.

www.ingramcontent.com/pod-product-compliance
Lightning Source LLC
Chambersburg PA
CBHW032109090426
42743CB00007B/291